Originally published as *Superbeesjes. Lawaaimakers*
in Belgium and the Netherlands by Clavis Uitgeverij, 2021
English translation from the Dutch by Clavis Publishing Inc., New York

Visit us on the Web at www.clavis-publishing.com.

Super Animals. The Loudest written by Reina Ollivier and Karel Claes,
and illustrated by Steffie Padmos

ISBN 978-1-60537-739-1

This book was printed in February 2022 at Nikara,
M. R. Štefánika 858/25, 963 01 Krupina, Slovakia.

First Edition
10 9 8 7 6 5 4 3 2 1

Clavis Publishing supports the First Amendment
and celebrates the right to read.

MIX
Paper from
responsible sources
FSC® C118365
FSC
www.fsc.org

SUPER
ANIMALS

THE
LOUDEST

Written by **Reina Ollivier** & **Karel Claes**
Illustrated by **Steffie Padmos**

Clavis

NEW YORK

Roaring, braying, croaking, or even booming,
some animals are really good at that!
It isn't always quiet in nature.
All that noise is there for a reason.
Animals want to say something with their sounds.
Sometimes they're looking for a partner.
Other times they're warning each other of danger.
Or they might be chasing intruders from their territory.
Animals use their voices or their bodies for that,
just like you can shout or clap your hands.
Do you think that only large animals make a lot of noise?
Then there are a few surprises in this book.
So listen up—here come the noisemakers!

CONTENTS

AFRICAN LION

Everyone calls me the "king of the animals." I have strong muscles and am proud of my beautiful mane. It's arranged in a wide circle around my neck. When I open my mouth to roar, all the animals become quiet.

Who am I?

Name: lion
Class: mammals

Noisemaker:
The African lion roars ferociously with its mouth wide open.

Legs:
4 sturdy, muscular legs

ears turn in different directions

Size:
males up to 4 feet (1.2 meters) shoulder height and up to 7 feet (2.1 meters) long, plus a tail of 3 feet (1 meter); females up to 3 feet (1 meter) shoulder height and up to 5 feet (1.5 meters) long

mouth can **open up to 11 inches (28 centimeters)**, with **powerful jaws** to break the neck of the prey

very **rough tongue** to lick dirt from its own fur and to scrape flesh from the bones of prey

4 canines (teeth) to tear off flesh and skin; they're **up to 3 inches (7 centimeters) long**

Habitat:
warm areas in Africa where there's a lot of grass, with trees here and there

only lions have a **mane**; lionesses do not

Food:
I'm a carnivore and eat mostly:

gazelles   wilde-beests   zebras

antelopes   buffaloes

Speed:
I can reach a top speed of 50 miles per hour, but I can't keep that up for long.

0   50 mph   60

Enemies:
I have no enemies among the animals.
My only enemies are:

humans

Cubs (young lions)
are sometimes attacked by:

hyenas   jackals   leopards

I'm the **leader**, and **no other lion** is allowed to **hunt** in our area. We live in a **pride** of **10 to 40 animals.** It consists mainly of **lionesses and cubs** and a few weaker males. **Male cubs** have to leave the pride after three years. They wander around on their own or form a **new group** with other males.

tail with tassel,
which is darker in color

Like a cat, I have **soft pads** under my paws. But as soon as I attack, my **supersharp nails** come out. They're almost 2 inches (5 centimeters) long, and I plant them deep into the flesh of my victim.

The **lionesses** are the **best hunters** because they're faster and more agile. But the animals they hunt are also fast and can run longer. That's why the lionesses **work together.** They sneak in a **semicircle** through the tall grass toward a herd of prey. When they're close, they sprint to a **weak animal** and attack it.

As the **leader,** I always get to **eat first.** Then come the other males, then the lionesses, and lastly the cubs. Most of the day, we **laze** in the grass or in a tree.

11

My enormous roar can be heard up to 5 miles (8 kilometers) away! I roar louder than the females and the weaker males in my pride. I usually do this in the morning when I wake up and in the evening before the lionesses go hunting. By roaring, I make it clear to the other lions in the neighborhood who the boss is here. That's how the lionesses know where I am and I remind them that I get to eat first if they're successful in the hunt.

I start with a long-drawn-out roar, which comes from very deep in my throat. It's followed by a series of shorter and faster roars.

But I also make a lot of other sounds. When I meet a lioness from my pride, I purr like a cat, but much louder. Then we're sweet to each other. We give gentle licks, rub against each other, and stroke each other with our paws. Our nails are retracted, of course!

When I'm angry or threatened by a young lion invading my territory, I hiss and snarl loudly.

ROOSTER

I stride across the yard with proud steps, for I'm the master of the henhouse. As soon as I wake up, I start crowing.

Who am I?

Name: rooster
Class: birds

Noisemaker:
He stretches his neck and loudly crows cock-a-doodle-doo!

Legs:
2 scaly legs

3 front toes and 1 back toe with sharp nails to scratch the ground and search for food

Size:
up to 28 inches (70 centimeters) tall; some species much smaller, barely 8 inches (20 centimeters) tall

1 pointy protrusion at the back of each foot, called a **spur**

long, curved **decorative feathers** in the tail

Food:
I like everything, even mice if I can catch them.

Habitat:
everywhere in the world, except at the North Pole and the South Pole

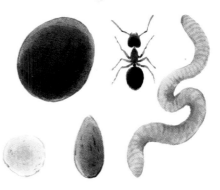

I also eat seeds, grass, fruit, vegetables, leaves, insects, and worms.

Speed:
My room to run in the farmyard often isn't big, but I can reach 9 miles per hour.

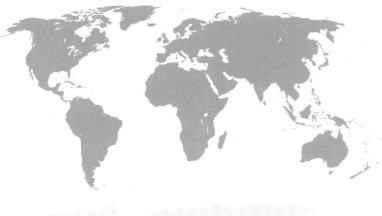

0   9 mph   60

Enemies:

foxes   wolves   rats   birds of prey   small predators

big, **bright red comb** on top of the head; long, **red wattles** on the ears and throat

I'm a **tamed** species and usually live **together with a number of hens.** If you want chicks, you need me. **Hens without a rooster** lay eggs, but **no chicks** come out of them.

Each animal knows its place in the group. We call that the **pecking order.** I get to peck at the food first and get the best place to sleep. We **sleep in a safe place,** on a stick or a branch, at least 3 feet (1 meter) above the ground.

There's only **one leader** in the henhouse, and that's me. Sometimes a young rooster wants to be the boss, and then we fight. I'm the strongest and win. When the **hens argue, I break them up.**

I **can't fly very far** because my wings are too small for my weight. I clean my feathers often, but not with water. I make a hole in the ground and take a **dust bath.** By doing that, I also scrub away the little insects that are on my skin.

17

I defend our territory against intruders. To show that I'm in charge, I frequently crow very loudly. You can hear me up to 1 mile (1.6 kilometers) away. Sometimes I do this before it gets light, and I repeat it several times during the day. A healthy, strong rooster like me crows often. That way, another rooster knows he has no chance here.

I can make many different sounds. When I find something delicious, I make a bell sound. That's how I invite the chickens to eat with me. When I see a bird of prey circling in the sky, I cackle to warn the others of the danger. When an enemy approaches by ground, I crow in a different way.

Enemies don't deter me. I spread my wings and lower them to the ground. That way, I look larger and more impressive. Then I walk menacingly toward the intruder and fly up to him cackling. Even with people, I dare to do that.

Every rooster has his own crowing sound. Young roosters need a lot of practice before they can crow correctly.

CICADA

When it's nice and warm during the summer months, you can hear me clearly. No, I'm not a cricket. That one rubs its wings together and makes much less noise than I do.

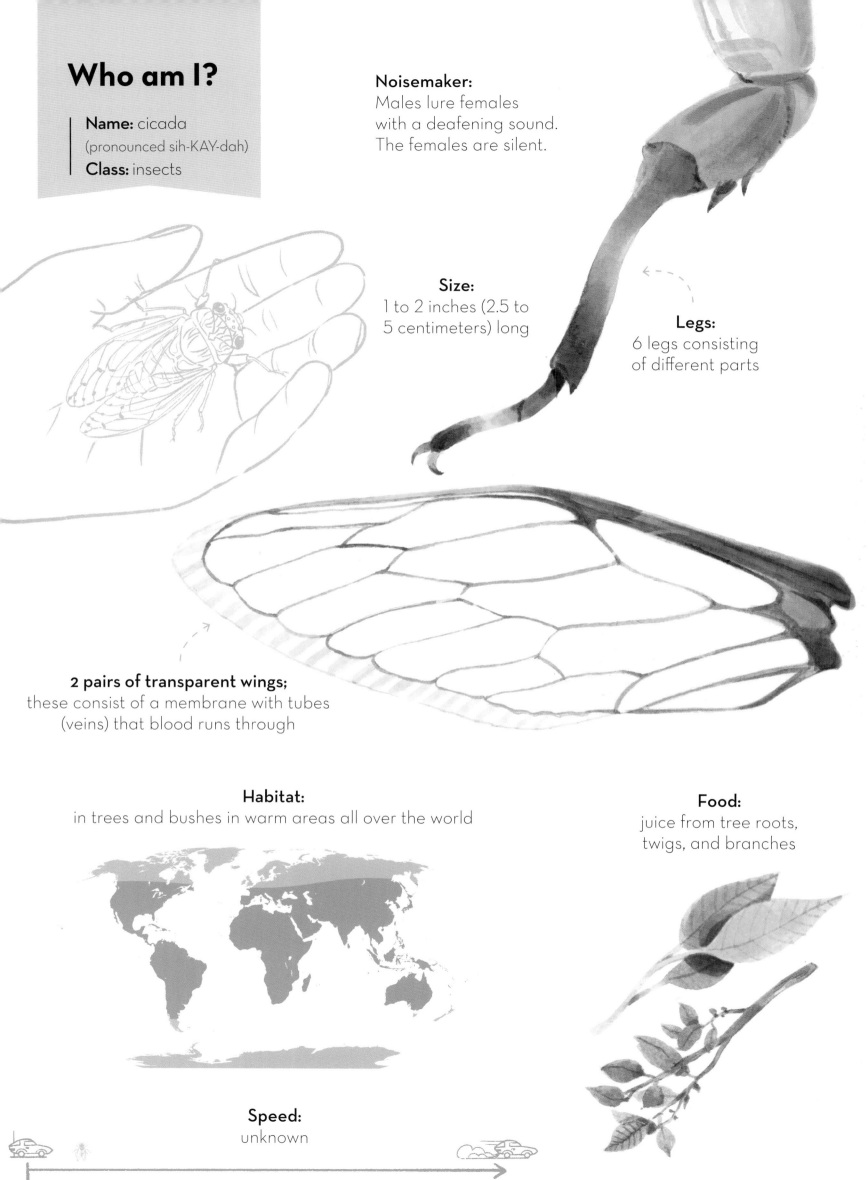

Who am I?

Name: cicada
(pronounced sih-KAY-dah)
Class: insects

Noisemaker:
Males lure females
with a deafening sound.
The females are silent.

Size:
1 to 2 inches (2.5 to
5 centimeters) long

Legs:
6 legs consisting
of different parts

2 pairs of transparent wings;
these consist of a membrane with tubes
(veins) that blood runs through

Habitat:
in trees and bushes in warm areas all over the world

Food:
juice from tree roots,
twigs, and branches

Speed:
unknown

0   ? mph   60

Enemies:

birds   snakes   salamanders   lizards   frogs   toads

spiders   predatory flies   wasps   grasshoppers   bats   squirrels

3 single eyes
on top of the head

You don't have to be afraid of me, as **I don't bite or sting.** I'm not a good jumper. I mainly use my wings to get around, but I only make **short flights** because those **wings** are **heavy.**

sucking beak

at the sides, **2 big, bulging eyes** that are composed of many tiny eyes

broad head with **2 short antennae**

When it gets too **hot** for other animals during the day, I feel **great.** I'm **constantly drinking** fluids, and these are secreted by my body to cool me down. That way, I **never get overheated.**

In North America, there are cicadas that crawl up out of the earth **only after 17 years.** Imagine that!

I began my life in an egg above the ground. When I hatched, I had **no wings** and was easy prey. With the claws of my front legs, I dug quickly **into the earth** to bury myself. I sucked juice from plant roots and grew vigorously. Meanwhile, I grew a **new shell** a few times. **After about a year,** I crawled out of the earth and up **into a tree.** There, I burst out of my shell for the last time. My **wings grew,** and my **new armor became hard.**

23

Behind my chest, I have a kind of drumhead on both sides of my abdomen. On the inside of that are vibrating plates, which I can push in and out of each other. That movement produces a series of clicking sounds. Because the clicking sounds follow each other quickly, it seems like a lingering tone.

In males, much of our abdomen is hollow. That reinforces the clicking I make with the vibrating plates. It's somewhat like the sound box of a guitar. My sound can be heard a mile (1.6 kilometers) away.

When you come looking for me, I stop making noise and crawl to the hidden side of the branch. I'm hard to see because my colors are adapted to the tree.

I use my clicking sounds to attract females.
Other males sing along with me, so we form a big choir.
Some cicadas in Africa and North America make lure sounds of 120 decibels. That's as loud as a rock concert!

DONKEY

I'm related to the horses and the zebras.
Maybe you recognize a few family traits?
There are many donkey species, but we
all have our own character and know
what we want. Hee-haw, hee-haw!

Who am I?

Name: donkey
Class: mammals

Legs:
4 sturdy legs
with hooves

Size:
36 to 55 inches (92
to 140 centimeters)
shoulder height

long, soft **ears** that can
move in a variety of directions,
independently of each other

Noisemaker:
A donkey that brays makes
a special sound that can
be heard very far away.

white muzzle and
mostly **gray body,**
sometimes brown
or black

Food:
preferably grass;
also plants and bushes

Habitat:
domestic donkeys, all over the world,
except in the polar regions; wild donkeys,
only in North Africa, parts of Asia, and Australia

Speed:
I can sprint briefly at a speed of 28 miles per hour.

0   28 mph   60

Enemies:
Domestic donkeys have no enemies. Enemies of donkeys in the wild:

bears   wolves   hyenas

short, **stiff mane** and **rough coat**

often a **dark stripe** across the back and shoulders

tail with a **tassel**

I'm **smaller and slower than a horse,** but I can **tolerate the heat and the cold better.** When it rains, I prefer to take shelter in a stable. People buy me because I'm **strong,** don't cost much, and require little care. They often use me to **transport** all kinds of things.

Donkeys are **herd animals** and like company. In my pasture, there are other donkeys, ponies, or goats.
You can always **pet** me because I **like** that. I'm a **friendly and smart** animal that likes to learn new things.

I stand **firmly on my legs** and can walk on **rocks** very well. That's also **good for my hooves,** because when I'm standing in a soft pasture, my hooves don't wear down enough.

When I **don't trust** something, **I freeze** and stay put. I don't run away like other animals. That's why they say I'm **stubborn** and won't listen.

I love to **roll in the dust.** I do it to shake off my winter coat, to chase away insects, and just to have fun. Don't get scared by the dust when you gently pat me on my neck or back!

My braying doesn't sound like music to your ears. You may even be startled the first time you hear it, because it sounds like I'm in trouble. I don't bray for a moment but for quite a while, sometimes up to 20 seconds at a time and a whole bunch of times in a row. I bray so loudly that you can hear me 1 to 2 miles (1.6 to 3.2 kilometers) away.

By braying, I talk to other donkeys. I can bray in many different ways. I do it loudly to show I'm strong, but quite softly when I'm greeting another donkey or a human. I bray a little plaintively when I feel alone and would like another donkey as a playmate. And watch out when I'm angry: then I sound very threatening. Besides braying, I can make other sounds: growling, snorting, squealing, and humming. But my braying is the most impressive.

Do you want to mimic my sound? Then breathe in deeply while saying "hee," and breathe out while saying "haw."

COMMON FROG

I live in and near the water. You can hear me clearly because I croak very loudly. But I'm really shy, and as soon as I feel threatened, I dive into the water with a big jump.

Who am I?

Name: common frog
Class: amphibian

Noisemaker:
Especially in the spring, frogs croak in groups to find their mate.

four toes on **front legs, five toes** on **hind legs**

Legs:
2 short front legs and 2 long, muscular hind legs

Size:
2 to 5 inches (5 to 12.7 centimeters); females larger than males

webbing on hind legs; these make the foot larger, so that the frog can push itself forward powerfully in the water

Habitat:
in and near canals, ponds, lakes, and streams in Europe

Food:
larvae, worms, flies, mosquitoes, beetles, cicadas, dragonflies, spiders, sometimes small mice

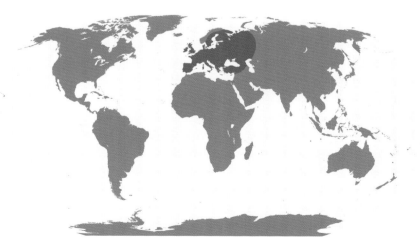

Speed:
My top speed is estimated at 5 miles per hour.

0   5 mph

Enemies:

herons   storks   birds of prey   badgers   otters   weasels   predatory fish   snakes   turtles

big eyes on the side of the head; can almost **see all around him**

smooth, **light green** upper body with **brown or black spots**

light **stripe** on the back

males have gray **vocal sacs** (strong skin that can stretch) on both cheeks

Our frog family was **created from two different types** of frogs: the pool frog and the marsh frog.

When I hatched from my **egg** in the water, I was a **tadpole.** I had a long **tail** and ate algae. Slowly, my legs and my body grew, and one day my tail fell off. From that moment on, I was a frog.

I can't warm myself **very well,** so I live in open water in a **sunny place.** On the bank or on the leaf of a water plant, I enjoy the warm sun.

I can **sit still** for so long that flies, spiders, and other insects I like forget that I'm there. They come right up to me. Then I quickly lash out with my **long, sticky tongue** and gulp them down. It happens so fast that you can't even see it.

My ears are under my skin, but I can **hear well,** even underwater. In the winter, it's too cold for me, and so I **hibernate.** I hide on land or at the bottom of the water.

35

I'm a male and have two vocal sacs, or bubbles. When I expand the bubbles, my croaking sounds much louder. I usually croak in the evening and at night. Especially during the mating season, I make myself heard because then I try to attract a female. The mating season starts in the second half of April and lasts until early July.

The warmer it is, the more energy I have and the louder and more often I croak. When one common frog near me starts croaking, I respond. All the other frogs do so too, and that way, we form a noisy choir of dozens of frogs. I love it, but some people can't sleep because of all the racket.

Do you think I just say "croak"? Then you should listen carefully. I make different sounds. When there's a threat, I sound an alarm so that all the nearby frogs can quickly hide in the water. When I'm looking for a female, I show with special and superloud croaking that I'm strong. And with a short guttural call, I indicate that this is my territory.

BLACK HOWLER MONKEY

I quietly search for food in the trees and don't like to be disturbed. By howling loudly, my troop and I tell everyone where our territory is. Then other monkeys stay away.

Who am I?

Name: black howler monkey
Class: mammals

Noisemaker:
The whole group howls in the morning and in the evening. The males make more noise than the females.

Size:
males 24 to 26 inches (60 to 65 centimeters) tall (without tail); females 20 inches (50 centimeters) tall

very hairy, except face, palms, soles, and bottom of the tail

Arms and legs:
2 long arms with 5 fingers on each hand; 2 long legs with 5 toes on each foot

Food:
leaves, fruits, flowers

Habitat:
the tropical rain forests of Bolivia, Brazil, Paraguay, and Argentina

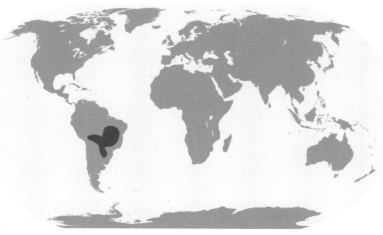

Speed:
All my food is nearby, so I move only about a quarter mile a day.

0 mph   60

Enemies:

people large birds of prey

People cut down trees in the rain forest, which causes us to lose our territory.

flexible tail that's approximately as **long** as the body

My family group consists of **5 to 8 monkeys,** but there are also groups of 20 monkeys. We live in the middle and **upper part of the trees. We rarely come down** because we find **all our food** in the **canopy.** There are enough fluids in our food, so we **don't need extra water.**

striking face with **long, lower jaw**

All black howler monkeys have a **golden-brown** coat **as a baby.** When I turned almost three years old, my coat turned black. Females don't change color.

I walk on all fours over the tree branches. Because my **tail** is **hairless at the bottom,** I can easily use it to **grab** things. It serves as a third arm or leg, and I sometimes hang from a branch with it.

Most of the day, **I rest.** In between, I look for food, we clean each other, and I play with the other monkeys. We're the **largest monkeys** in the **South American rain forests.**

My call resembles the roar of a lion or the barking of a dog. I have a long lower jaw and a large hyoid bone at the back of my mouth. Together, these form a hollow space. Think of an empty room or a tunnel. Every sound is echoed in it. My howl sounds twice as loud because of this!

Together, we can produce a volume of up to 140 decibels. That's as much as a plane taking off 164 feet (50 meters) away from you. If you know that your hearing can be damaged from 120 decibels, you better stay away from our concert! You can hear our howling choir up to 3 miles (5 kilometers) away. We howl early in the morning and toward the evening to tell other groups where we are, so they'll stay away. Because we have no fixed territory and sometimes move to a different eating place, we howl so that we never run into each other unexpectedly. We don't want to fight to defend our eating place. In our food, there's just enough energy to get through the day. Fighting requires too much effort.

EUROPEAN GREEN WOODPECKER

You can see me sitting on the lawn early in the morning. As soon as you come closer, I fly away with a shrill laugh.

Who am I?

Name: European green woodpecker

Class: birds

Noisemaker:
The green woodpecker has a loud, shrill call and hammers softly on trees.

Legs:
2 legs with **sharp claws;** each leg has two toes forward and two backward

Size:
12 to 14 inches (30 to 34 centimeters) long from beak to tip of the tail; males and females the same size

When **flying,** I flap my wings three or four times and then fold them up for a moment each time I flap. That way, I let myself glide through the air in a **wavy motion.**

wingspan 16 to 16.5 inches (40 to 42 centimeters)

Habitat:
forest edges, orchards, and large gardens with lots of grass in Europe and western Asia

Food:
ants, insects, spiders

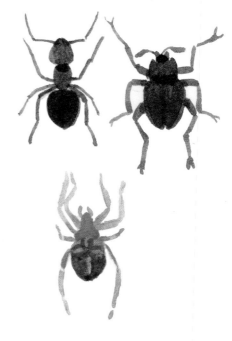

Speed:

0   30 mph   60

striking **red crown** and **black mask around the eyes**

strong beak 2 inches (5 centimeters) long

very long tongue; up to 4 inches (10 centimeters) outside the beak

With **four toes** on each foot, I **hook myself to a tree.** The stiff feathers of my short **tail** give me **extra support.** I always keep my **head up.** When I want to go down the trunk, I just take a few steps backward.

When I don't find an abandoned **nest** in a hollow tree, I chop a hole out myself. I choose a **tree with soft wood** and use my nest for many years in a row.

males have a **red stripe under each eye**

I **love ants** and also like their eggs and larvae. That's why I sit on the ground more often than other woodpecker species. I drill deep **holes in the lawn** with my beak, and all the treats stick to my **long, sticky tongue.** I eat about **2,000 ants a day.** Winters with lots of snow aren't for me because then I can't reach the ants and have to find other food.

I'm very shy, and at the slightest threat, I fly away laughing loudly. It sounds something like "kluuk-kluuk-kluuk-kluuk." My call echoes in nature, and you may have been startled by it already. It's a very striking sound.

I also make myself heard fiercely when I defend my territory and when I want the attention of a female. During the breeding season, we form a pair, but the rest of the year, I prefer to be alone.

I don't tap on trees as much as other woodpeckers because my favorite food is in the earth. Sometimes I tap a tree to find insects. I hammer quickly, with no set rhythm. My head is specially built, so I never get a headache from hammering. I have a thick skull, strong neck muscles, and a sturdy beak. My skull is like a bicycle helmet that absorbs the shocks.

My long tongue rolls up inside my head. It's like a safety belt around my brain. I can tap 20 times a second without getting dizzy.

PISTOL SHRIMP

Do you think my name is a joke? No way!
Underwater, I create a loud boom and a flash
of light with a single shot. I'm a small creature,
but I have a powerful weapon.

Who am I?

Name: pistol shrimp
Class: crustaceans

small claw with **pincher** at the end to catch and eat prey

large claw with **weapon** to kill prey; at least as big as **half the body**

Noisemaker:
Pistol shrimp stun and kill their food by firing a loud, explosive shot of water from their claw.

Size:
1 to 2 inches (2.5 to 5 centimeters), not including antennae

Legs:
8 walking legs and 2 claws of unequal size

Habitat:
both in temperate and tropical seawater and some species even in cold water

Food:
shrimp, little crabs, gobies, sea worms

Speed:
I don't cover much distance, but I shoot my prey at a speed of 60 miles per hour!

0   60

Enemies:

groupers   wrasses   lionfish   triggerfish   hawkfish

There are more than **600 pistol shrimp species.**
We live in **oyster beds, coral reefs,** or plains on the
seafloor overgrown with **seagrass.** Some pistol shrimp
live together by the hundreds in **sponges.**

sees almost nothing but
uses **antennae** to navigate
its surroundings

When my **big claw** is **torn off,** something very
special happens. My **little claw grows** into
a big claw with a weapon. And in the place
of the torn-off claw grows a small claw with
a pincher. My gun just changes sides!

With our big claw, we **shoot water bubbles** at **food.**
But we **don't see much,** and that makes us an **easy
target** for enemies. That's why we **work together**
with others. I chose a **goby,** a lively little fish that
sees very well. To hide, I boom with my big claw,
and that way I **drill** a **hole** in the sand or in a rock.
The goby can hide there as well. I keep our
residence clean, and the **goby** provides
surveillance. We stay **close to each other.**
As soon as the goby sees an enemy,
it moves. I notice this thanks to my
antennae, and then I flee too.

53

My big claw consists of two parts connected by a joint, just like your thumb is connected to your other fingers. I lift the upper part of my claw and drop it onto the lower part like a hammer superfast. That's how a gun works too.

I don't shoot a bullet but an air bubble in the water. Because of the high speed at which I shoot, that bubble heats up to as much as 9,000 degrees Fahrenheit. That's almost as hot as the sun! The bubble can't handle that heat, swells up, and explodes. That explosion causes a huge shock wave in the water and kills nearby animals. And that's how I get food.

The bubble explodes with a boom that has a sound of 210 decibels. That's much more noise than a real gunshot, which is about 160 decibels. My shot also produces a flash of light, but you can only see it with a special camera, because everything happens in less than a second!

TAWNY OWL

I live in the forest and am awake at night.
When everyone is asleep, I let out my call,
which many people find eerie. With my wings
spread, I glide silently through the trees.

Who am I?

Name: tawny owl
Class: birds

Noisemaker:
The tawny owl breaks the silence of the night with hooting calls.

Legs:
2 sturdy legs with sharp nails; each leg has two toes forward and two backward

Size:
14 to 17 inches (36 to 43 centimeters) tall; females are larger than males

dark feathers around flattened **face;** can **turn head** almost all the way around

wingspan 31.5 to 41 inches (80 to 105 centimeters)

ears hidden between the feathers on sides of the head; flat shape of face leads sound to the ears, which **aren't at the same height to hear better**

weighs **only 1 pound (500 grams);** has **mostly a lot of feathers**

Habitat:
in forests, parks, and gardens in large parts of Europe, Asia, and North Africa

Food:
mice, young rabbits, frogs, earthworms, fish, birds, insects

Speed:

0   50 mph   60

Enemies:

foxes   weasels   buzzards   eagles   hawks   larger owls

At night, I go **hunting.** High up in my lookout post, I listen to what moves in the forest. I **hear very well,** ten times better than you. When I hear an animal below me, I fly to it through the trees. I do that **very quietly** but **at lightning speed.**

While eating, I **swallow everything,** including feathers and bones. What my stomach can't digest, I cough up later. You can find these **pellets** near the tree where I have my nest. You can tell from them what I've eaten.

When there are **young** in the nest, I'll **defend** them. I even dare to attack people when they come too close. But after four months, I send the young out of the nest, and they have to find their own territory.

I usually make my **nest** in a **hollow tree trunk,** high above the ground. Sometimes I use an abandoned nest of other birds. I stay in the **same neighborhood all my life,** with the **same partner.** As a result, I know a lot about every little spot.

You won't easily see me in the forest because my feathers are the color of branches and dry leaves. But at dusk and at night, you can hear me well.

I call "hoooooooooot" in a trembling voice, and that sounds spooky. Only the males make a sound like that, and it's slightly different with each male. The male that can keep this up the longest is considered the strongest of all the owls in the neighborhood. Females then often respond with "kie-wiek, kie-wiek."

I know the sound of every owl that lives nearby. So, I immediately know that an intruder is approaching when I hear an unfamiliar call.

With all kinds of sounds and different pitches, we pass messages. I have a cry to tell my female, who's breeding on the nest, that I'm coming with food. When there's a threat, I sound the alarm with shrill screeches. When another owl wants to invade my territory, I screech very loudly to scare it away.

In the fall, owls are noisier because the young animals are looking for a territory for themselves. They try to claim it by hooting loudly. Sometimes they have to fight with young owls from other nests.